SCHIRMER'S LIBRARY
OF MUSICAL CLASSICS

Vol. 2089

FRIEDRICH DOTZAUER

Exercises for the Violoncello
Books 1 and 2

ISBN 978-1-4234-9088-3

G. SCHIRMER, Inc.

DISTRIBUTED BY

HAL•LEONARD®
CORPORATION
7777 W. BLUEMOUND RD. P.O. BOX 13819 MILWAUKEE, WI 53213

www.schirmer.com
www.halleonard.com

PREFACE

Since their appearance, the Violoncello Études by Dotzauer—who was born June 26, 1783, and died March 6, 1860—have ranked high among works of their class and, by reason of their intrinsic practical utility, have successfully maintained their position. It therefore seems entirely justifiable to bring out a new edition in line with modern requirements.

Dotzauer's numerous études are an outgrowth of mature experience in teaching, and display such a full and comprehensive understanding of the peculiarities of the instrument, that their well-earned place in the literature of violoncello-instruction would seem to be assured for the future also.

After careful consideration I reached the conclusion that a satisfactory new edition would be something different, in many respects, from a mere reprint of the original editions. I felt that the usefulness of these Études under present conditions would be greatly enhanced by a judicious selection from and rearrangement of the great mass of material; numerous mistakes had to be corrected, numbers of comparatively small value and utility had to be eliminated, and those of real importance and usefulness arranged in progressive order and clear classification, so that the present edition might be used as a supplement to any and every Method for Violoncello. My aim being not merely to promote technical efficiency, but to refine the taste and increase the capacity for shading and diversifying the tone, I have added—besides the needful fingerings, directions for the portions of the bow to be employed, and the establishment of the correct notation—marks of interpretation (expression and tempo) throughout; these latter, in earlier editions, were almost entirely wanting.

I hope that these admirable Études may now go forth in this more attractive garb, to promote and facilitate the difficult study of the Violoncello.   JOHANNES KLINGENBERG

Contents

Book 1 (Nos. 1-34)

Contents

Book 2 (Nos. 35–62)

Signs and Abbreviations

⊓   Down - Bow

V   Up - Bow

WB   Whole Bow

UH   Upper Half of Bow

LH   Lower Half of Bow

N   At the Nut

M   Middle of Bow

Pt.   At the Point

⌐   Keep the finger on the note indicated until the line ends

Exercises for Violoncello
Book I, Nos. 1–34
113 Études for Violoncello

Friedrich Dotzauer
(1783–1860)

Allegro

10

Allegro

4

Allegro

6

Another bowing

Moderato

7

Allegro

8

13

Allegro

13

14 Allegro

Different Bowings

Other Bowings

19

Allegro

20

Allegro non troppo

22

Allegro ma non troppo

25

Arpeggios

Other Bowings

34

27   Allegro

28

Allegro non troppo

30

Allegro

31

44

Allegro non troppo

32

Allegro non troppo

Allegro non tanto

34

p dolce

cresc.

mf

Exercises for Violoncello
Book II, Nos. 35–62
113 Études for Violoncello

Friedrich Dotzauer
(1783–1860)

Allegro

37

Allegro

38

Allegro

39

Allegro

41

Allegro

43

Allegro

44

Allegro

45

Allegro

46

Allegro assai

48

Allegro

49

Poco allegro

50

Allegro non troppo

51

Allegro

52

Allegro non troppo

54

Allegro non tanto

56

Andante con moto

59

Allegro

60